I Love You as BIG as the World

For Joey and Ciara ~ two little ones who are a big part of my world ~ D B

For little Levi Louis ~ T W

Original edition published in English by Little Tiger Press, an imprint of Magi Publications, London, England, 2008.

ISBN-13: 978-0-545-16511-2
ISBN-10: 0-545-16511-3

Published by Scholastic Inc., 557 Broadway, New York, NY 10012, by arrangement with Good Books. SCHOLASTIC and associated logos are trademarks and/or registered trademarks of Scholastic Inc.

12 11 10 9 8 7 6 5 4 3 10 11 12 13 14/0

Printed in the U.S.A. 40

First Scholastic printing, April 2009

I Love You as BIG as the World

David Van Buren

Tim Warnes

SCHOLASTIC INC.
New York Toronto London Auckland Sydney
Mexico City New Delhi Hong Kong Buenos Aires

I love you as

big as the

world.

I love you as deep as the sea.

I love you as

bright

as the sun.

I love you.

And I know you love me!

I love you

as blue as the sky.

I love you as long as the days.

I love you as

high as the mountain top.

I love you in so many ways!

I love you as strong

as the wind.

I love you as soft as the dew.

I love you as far as a star.

I love you because . . .

. . . you are

you!